FAVOUR

YOUR KEY TO A LASTING SUCCESS IN LIFE

BRIAN AMOATENG

Unless otherwise indicated, Scripture quotations are from the King James Version (KJV) and the New International Version (NIV) of the Holy Bible. Scripture quotation identified NIV are from, The New Scofield Study Bible, New International Version, Copyright © 1984 by Oxford University Press, Inc. Scripture quotation identified KJV are from the New Marked Reference Bible, the King James Version, Copyright © 1964, 1972 by ZODERVAN PUBLISHING HOUSE.

FAVOUR

ISBN: 978-9988-8568-1-6
Copyright ©2013 by Brian Amoateng

Edited by:
Claude A. Mann, Sr. [+233-243-259-634, Diamond-Pen Writings]

Designed, Printed and Published by:
Kharis Books
(The book publishing unit of Kharis Media Limited)

P. O. Box Co 2704, Tema-Ghana
+233 (0)303 309956
+233 (0)544 000042
+233 (0)245 202626

For your personal copy of this, information about other books by author and bulk purchase please contact:

All rights reserved. No part of this publication may be reproduced, stored or transmitted in any form or by any means, electronic or mechanical, including photocopy, recording or any information storage or retrieval system, without permission, in writing, from the author except for brief quotations in books, articles and critical reviews.

CONTENTS

Dedications		 v
Acknowledgements		 vi
INTRODUCTION		 vii
1.	WHAT IS FAVOUR?	 13
2.	FAVOUR COMES FIRST AS 'SPIRITUAL BLESSINGS'	 17
3.	DIMENSIONS OF FAVOUR	 25
4.	PEOPLE THAT ATTRACTED GOD'S FAVOUR IN THE BIBLE	 33
5.	FAVOUR, MERCY AND GRACE	 39
6.	BENEFITS OF FAVOUR	 49
7.	REMAINING IN THE FAVOUR OF GOD	 63
	CONCLUSTION	 71

Dedication

I dedicate this book to my good friend, Honourable Obuobia Darko-Opoku. Thank you for always being there for me. God bless you.

Acknowledgements

I want to thank God for giving me the insight and revelation to write this book.

I want to thank Pastor Claude A. Mann of Diamond Pen Writings for his guidance in developing this manuscript. You are indeed a great editor.

To Pastor Akin Benson and the family of RCCG SUN CITY PARISH (Abuja, Nigeria) for your love to my ministry. Not forgetting Pastor Kola Abawonse of RCCG ABUJA, thank you sir for everything.

To all my sons and daughters in ministry; God keep all of you.

Finally, to my Publisher, Mr Randy Osae Bediako, (CEO of Kharis Media Ltd, Ghana) and your entire team. God bless you.

Introduction

"To give special regard to or to show exceptional kindness to someone this is, to give preferential treatment to an individual."

- DAVID REAGAN

FINDING FAVOUR WITH GOD AND MAN IS THE GREATEST PRIVILEGE any person can ever enjoy here on earth! In case you do not grasp what I mean, just imagine that you have been informed that Her Royal Majesty, Queen Elizabeth of England, has given you a special invitation to attend a dinner party in her royal palace. Tell me how you will feel that day? How will you receive the message and what kind of preparation would you make to honour such a high-class invitation? I am sure you first will not believe it because you have no royal connection to Queen Elizabeth.

YOU WILL THEN BEGIN TO THINK DEEPLY and reflect and ask yourself "What have I done to deserve such an invitation? How come, me, an ordinary me, is being invited to such a royal treat?" No matter how long you ask yourself, the plain truth is, you do not deserve that honour, yet you have been selected and invited. It is purely a privilege and not a right. You have been singled out among many thousands, if not millions or billions, to enjoy such a great company.

Then comes the ultimate moment; you are ushered through the top-class security zone. Finally you are face to face with the most powerful queen on earth, Queen Elizabeth of England! You bow before her in obeisance and express the greatest of reverence and humility before her. She ushers you to a seat and introduces you to the august audience. What a great privilege!

THIS IS WHAT THE BIBLE CALLS 'FAVOUR BEFORE MAN' and I see the Lord giving you such a great privilege today, as you read this book. You are about to have a personal encounter with the King of kings and the Lord of lords! I see God singling you out of your family and like Gideon, He picks you out of the family, which is the poorest of the poor and the least of the least clan of the tribe, and puts your feet on a higher ground! That is what the favour of God is and you qualify to experience it today!

DAVID SHOWED MEPHIBOSHETH FAVOUR AND KINDNESS

DAVID HAD ASCENDED THE THRONE OF ISRAEL. He then displayed his most admirable spirit: instead of using his royal power tyrannically, David rather put it to a most noble use, by returning good for evil. He extended forgiveness to the only surviving descendant of his arch-foe, King Saul. Read what David did:

> *"And David said, 'Is there yet any that is left of the house of Saul, that I may show him kindness for Jonathan's sake?"*
> *(2 Samuel 9:1)*

Now, behind the noble magnanimity David exercised towards the last descendant of his arch-enemy, King Saul, we can perceive the shining forth of God's glory and the beauty of His grace towards the fallen and sinful people on earth. Those who are the most indebted to the divine favour are the ones God shows His goodwill and generosity! No wonder, awful sinners become so humble and express deep gratitude, praise, admiration and adoration unto God for showing them undeserved kindness! Have you stopped and thanked God for His goodwill towards you?

When the poor outcast and physically-challenged son of Jonathan was brought from Lodebar to Jerusalem, he was not only shown kindness, but David accorded him a place in the king's family and Mephibosheth was given a seat at David's own table! That is favour at work because Mephibosheth never deserved that high honour because of the sins of Saul, his grandfather. I can imagine how he must have felt and how he was dumbfounded and could hardly find the right words to express his gratitude unto David.

We also ought to go through this state of pure gratitude, when as slaves of sin and captives of Satan, Christ set us free from sin and Satan's power of dominion over us. Our joy and surprise grow even greater when God makes us

His sons and joint-heirs with His Son, Jesus Christ! Like Mephibosheth, we get lost in wonderment! I know what am saying because I experienced it when I got born again, and till today, each morning, I get lost in wonderment as I thank God, praise Him and adore Him for His grace and mercies that are renewed each morning.

In fact, it will require eternity for me to truly render unto God all the worship that He is entitled! May you also develop this awesome attitude towards God and His grace, mercies and divine favour shall continually flow towards you. Like Mephibosheth, you shall daily sit and eat with the King of kings at His banqueting table and revel in His love that is over you and envelops you in His glory!

I HEAR GOD CALLING YOUR NAME NOW! May you respond and be connected to His goodwill and His kindness. May your life never be the same as you read this book about favour! May favour locate you, even if you are imprisoned in a far place called Lodebar – which literally means, 'a place of no communication.' No matter how you see yourself as an outcast or undeserving of God's blessings, change your mind now! Begin to see yourself as the target of God's blessings. Know that, you can never save yourself, so you need the Saviour. Receive Him and He shall grant you His divine favour, which is granted out of His goodwill and not from justice. No matter how dark your past is, Jesus Christ has paid for your redemption with His precious blood and

His favour is awaiting you. So just open up, release your faith in Him and He shall grant you His grace, mercies and favour!

> *"For thou, Lord, wilt bless the righteous; with favour wilt thou compass him as with a shield."*
>
> **Psalm 5:12**

My dear reader, if you are already born again and in Christ, then begin to walk in the knowledge of His salvation that He granted you free of charge and without cost to you! Know that He has approved you and has made you His favourite. He has blessed you with all heavenly blessings. But you can only access and enjoy His blessings when you understand the subject of favour and how to walk in it. So read further and enjoy favour before God and before man! You are God's favourite! Never forget this!

It is important to find favour with both man and God but even better to find favour with God! This is the message you shall encounter throughout this book: how to connect to the favour of God and by His favour, become successful and prosperous in all you do for His glory. Enjoy the journey through this book with me! Shalom!

PASTOR BRIAN AMOATENG

President, Brian Jones Outreach Ministries [BJOM]
London, United Kingdom

CHAPTER 1

WHAT IS FAVOUR?

"And Jesus increased in wisdom and in stature and in favour with God and man."

Luke 2:52, ESV

TO FAVOUR MEANS TO GIVE SPECIAL REGARD TO; or to treat with goodwill. It also means, to show exceptional kindness to someone. Sometimes, it means to show extra kindness in comparison to the treatment of others. That is called preferential treatment. For example, Esther received royal favour above all the other virgins (Esther 2:17). It is from this use of favour that we get the word, favourite. The greatest favours are shown to the favourite.

AS A YOUNG MAN, JESUS GREW IN FAVOUR. Abel, Seth, Noah, Joseph, Moses, Ruth, Esther, and David, they all had something in common: they all found the favour of God and that manifested as they had favour with men as well. Favour always begins with God. Favour belongs to the unique realm of divinity when God pours out His goodness on humanity. He turns negative situations around, increases faith for moving mountains, blesses people who were not blessed, shows His grace, mercies and goodwill to people who least qualified or expected such breakthroughs.

However, favour is not always used in a comparative way toward others. It sometimes simply means that the one favoured is shown kindness and treated with a generosity and goodwill far beyond what would normally be expected. This is generally the favour that we receive from the Lord. We are treated much better than we could expect. Every believer is favoured to some measure.

WHAT DOES IT MEAN TO BE 'FAVOURED'?

THE VINES COMPLETE EXPOSITORY DICTIONARY OF OLD AND NEW TESTAMENT WORDS defines the word "favour" as follows: "goodwill, acceptance, will, desire or pleasure." It can also be defined as the condition of being held in regard or approval or support. Webster's dictionary defines favour as: "friendly or kind regard." It is an "unfair partiality" showed a person – who becomes a favourite. It is an "attractiveness or special preference" shown to a person. It is an "act or magnanimity, benevolence or a kindness for" and "endorsing" of a person who is deemed as favoured by a higher authority.

According to *Bakers' Evangelical Dictionary of Biblical Theology*, favour is "gaining approval, acceptance or special benefit or blessing." Yes, favour is having unlimited access

> **FAVOUR IS...**
>
> *"To give special regard to or to show exceptional kindness to someone this is, to give preferential treatment to an individual."*
>
> - DAVID REAGAN

to God's blessings, when you have not worked for or merited that flow of blessing towards you. Any blessing that you get as a result of your sweat is not favour; it is the result of your diligence. Favour bypasses hard work!

FAVOUR IS A MENTALITY AND A MINDSET

WHEN ONE WALKS IN FAVOUR, one sees oneself to be blessed and treated preferentially. Even when there is no outward or physical manifestation of the blessing he is blessed with, a favoured person carries a grace that makes others see him as an honourable person – as in the case of Jabez. Thus, a favoured person has a kind of mentality that makes him see himself as blessed and highly favoured. He sees God showing him preferential treatment. Do you have that attitude? Then you are counted as a favoured person!

BISHOP O. A. BERNARD of the Praise Valley Temple Churches Worldwide defines favour simply as: "being beautified in the spirit." That simply means that, favour begins as an attitude and it is an attitude that is usually called 'sweet spirit.' Have you heard someone described as having a 'sweet spirit'? Then that person carries the virtue of favour in him. Indeed, favour is what makes one attractive in the spirit, as we manifest who we are inside outwardly. You cannot carry the virtue of favour in you and fail to show it in your actions! Bishop Bernard states further that "favour is a spiritual blessing from God which causes you to get physical things in your life".

> *"Never take lightly the favors others bestowed on your life, it is a big thing in a small world."*
>
> **DR. MIKE MURDOCK**

The truth is, when God favours a person, it reflects on them and makes them smell of grace, elegance, brilliance, beauty and goodness. That makes them attractive and brings good things into their life without effort. When you walk in divine favour, it means God has approved you, endorsed you, regarded you highly, preferred you among many, and has shown you unstoppable kindness.

My dear reader, pause now and convince yourself that you are favoured by God, your Father. Begin to feel it resonate in your body. Rest assured that it is the will of God to give you special privileges. Yes, the favour of God will cause people to go out of their way to bless you and do you good without even knowing why they are doing that! Note that God is showering all these blessings on you so that, the more you are blessed, the more you can be a blessing unto others too! Never forget this!

CHAPTER 2

FAVOUR COMES FIRST AS 'SPIRITUAL BLESSINGS'

"Blessed be the God and Father of our Lord Jesus Christ, who has blessed us with every spiritual blessing in the heavenly places in Christ..."

Ephesians 1:3

GOD'S FAVOUR COMES FIRST, IN THE FORM OF SPIRITUAL BLESSINGS, rather than in material blessings. Apostle Paul expatiates on this more in his letter to the Church of Ephesus. After a brief salutation, Paul began his letter to the Ephesians with a lengthy description of the spiritual blessings we have in Christ. These blessings, covered in verses 3 to 14, are all one sentence in the original Greek! This was to lay emphasis on how deeply and greatly God has favoured His children, who are in Christ Jesus.

Paul begins by blessing God for the blessings He has given

us. Paul describes these blessings as "spiritual" blessings, and blessings that are in "heavenly places," meaning the blessings are not physical or material. Many preachers and teachers today teach that God's "blessing" is physical or even monetary. However, God's blessings first come as a divine approval of: **hope, peace, good well-being,** and an **abundant life**. These are far better blessings than just money or health.

> *"Blessed be the God and Father of our Lord Jesus Christ, who has blessed us with every spiritual blessing in the heavenly places in Christ..."*
>
> **EPHESIANS 1:3**

The truth is God blesses us with a spiritual blessing which will enable us to get the physical thing we need such as money, a car, a house etc. That is why the wise man in Proverbs stated that the blessings of the Lord once it comes on you will make you rich (rich in the sense of material needs).

"The blessing of the Lord makes one rich, and He adds no sorrow with it."
(Proverbs 10:22, NKJV)

WE CAN GROW IN FAVOUR BOTH WITH GOD AND WITH MAN

THE CHILD SAMUEL HAD THAT DOUBLE-FAVOUR (1 Samuel 2:26) and so was the Child Jesus (Luke 2:52). The phrase, 'to find favour in the eyes of,' or, 'in the sight of,' originates from the Old Testament. Every child of God should desire and seek to have favour in the eyes of the Lord. As God showers His favour on us, we should know that it is our responsibility to grow in that favour as we faithfully live for the Lord. As we walk in faithfulness to God and in His favour, He grants us favour in the sight of men. As King Solomon wrote in the Book of Proverbs, thus favour, coupled with excellence, skilfulness and diligence in what we do, we are ushered before persons of great dignity and in higher places:

> *"Do you see a man who excels in his work? He will stand before kings; He will not stand before unknown men." (Proverbs 22:29, NKJV)*

GOD REWARDS EXCELLENCE AND DILIGENCE

WHAT DO YOU HAVE TO DO TO ENSURE THAT FAVOUR FLOWS TOWARDS YOU? Diligence is one of the major keys. Whenever you put in efforts to make the best in you come out to His glory, God blesses you and makes you His favourite and makes people notice you. So favour and diligence walk together. Favour is attracted by people with excellent spirit. However, let me admit here that this is not to be looked upon as some sort of secret formula for getting everything we want!

> *"Seest thou a man diligent in his business? He shall stand before kings; he shall not stand before mean men."*
> **(Proverbs 22:29, KJV)**

For His own sovereign purposes, God sometimes takes those He loves so much through unusual trials. Job is the primary example and similar instances also happen in the lives of many godly people today. However, if we continually draw closer to the Lord and we choose to dwell in His presence and walk in His grace, He grants us His peace and His favour. He ensures that our dark moments give birth to better times, and His joy replaces our sorrows, as the Psalmist sang:

> *"For His anger endureth but a moment, and in His favour is life; weeping may endure for a night, but joy cometh in the morning."*
> *(Psalm 30:5, 21st Century King James Version)*

FAVOUR SURROUNDS YOU LIKE A MAGNETIC FIELD

FAVOUR IS LIKE THE CENTRIPETAL FORCE THAT PULLS EVERYTHING TOWARDS IT. Are you God's child? Then know that you are surrounded by favour from the Creator of the entire universe and the master of everything. You are a prince and of royal family, so all the wealth of the Kingdom is at your disposal! To be favoured is to be at the right place at the right time, with the right attitude to receive the right blessings from God and from people God empowers to favour you. Favour is enjoying the sorrow-free blessings of God as King Solomon testified and wrote in the Book of Proverbs:

> *"The blessing of the LORD brings wealth,*

without painful toil for it."
(Proverbs 10:22, NIV)

FAVOUR IS THE STATE OF BEING APPROVED OR HELD IN HIGH REGARD

"You will arise and have compassion on Zion, for it is time to show favour to her; the appointed time has come." (Psalm 102:13)

FAVOUR IS AT WORK, when people just seem to want to help you and seek nothing in return. Favour is being a victor not a victim. Favour is the grace of God manifesting physically in your life. Favour is the gift of eternal life that manifests as an abundant life in you that brings you peace of mind. Favour is the assurance you get in your heart that God has forgiven you of all your sins and granted His grace, His mercies and His goodness, when you least deserve it.

FAVOUR IS KNOWING THAT JESUS CHRIST DIED ON THE CROSS for our sins and walking in that salvation freely, knowing that it is not by our works that we are saved and redeemed from sin's power. Favour is being confident of the truth that, you are strong in the Lord and in the power of His might. Favour is being fully aware that God has called you and has given you His Spirit and empowered you with His spiritual gifts to enable you fulfil your God-given destiny on earth. Favour is praying for, seeking and finding a good wife in your youth!

> *"He who finds a wife finds a good thing, and gets favour from the Lord."*
> *(Proverbs 18:22)*

You are walking in favour when you are aware that God has given you everything you need to make it in this life. Favour is walking in the knowledge that, no one can harm you, and that God has given His angels charge over you and that they will not permit your feet to stumble. Favour is being a friend of God. Favour is being able to breathe freely and enjoying good health and vitality.

FAVOUR IS HAVING TRUE PEACE IN THE HEART, even in the midst of turmoil and upheavals of the world around you. Favour is what grants you fortitude and inner stay to face troubles and go through fires and floods without losing your cool. Favour is walking in the knowledge and gratitude that God is the source of every good and perfect gift you enjoy here on earth.

> *"Every good and perfect gift is from above, coming down from the Father of the heavenly lights, who does not change like shifting shadows." (James 1:17)*

I WOULD NEVER WANT TO LIVE WITHOUT THE FAVOUR OF GOD ON MY LIFE! The Bible does clearly state that we need to be obedient to Him and do everything we know to do to receive His favour. Just as you would not show unusual favour to your own children if they were misbehaving or disobeying you, God is no different with us as His children. Note therefore that, favour is not automatic, though it is freely given. Some caution must therefore be taken when you desire God's favour.

Having a willing heart, an obedient attitude and a prayerful desire is very necessary. You must ask, seek and knock at heaven's door till it opens to you. As you do these with a sincere heart and with faith, God begins to pour out His blessings and gifting towards you in a dramatic way.

> *"May the favour of the Lord our God rest on us; establish the work of our hands for us - yes, establish the work of our hands."*
>
> **Psalm 90:17, NIV**

Have you been missing the sweet taste of God's goodwill in your life? Begin to pray for and desire God's favour. Stop doing warfare that are the preserve of angels and let God fight your battles for you. Seek rather to enjoy good fellowship with your heavenly Father in prayer, thanksgiving, and praise and in worship. Continue to commune with God and have faith in Him. Keep sowing good seeds. Then sooner than later, God shall visit you and you shall reap God's favour, which is in abundance in the heavenly realms, waiting for you to position yourself to access them!

MAY FAVOUR BE OUR PORTION!

May you continually increase in wisdom and in spiritual stature, pleasing God in all you do, and in so doing, finding favour with both God and man! Now, before you read the next chapter, spare some minutes in quality prayer thanking God for His unmerited and undeserving favour, mercies, and grace that He is pouring into your life! May you choose to live a life of total obedience, unalloyed faith in God, pleasing Him in all you do, and He shall bless you with overwhelming favour! Amen!

CHAPTER 3

DIMENSIONS OF FAVOUR

"For You, O Lord, will bless the righteous; with favour You will surround him as with a shield."

Psalm 5:12, NKJV

FAVOUR COMES IN DIFFERENT DIMENSIONS. As we saw in the previous chapter, favour comes to us from God and He first sends us favour as 'spiritual blessings' which physically manifest as "favour before God" and "favour before men." Favour begins as a seed that is sown, and with good watering and nurturing, soon it begins to sprout and show signs of flowers and budding of fruit.

You see the evidence that you are growing in favour when you observe with joy that things are turning round in your life. When favour is increasing in your life, you begin to evidence that you are regaining in a day what Satan has stolen from you in years! Indeed, God does not want to withhold anything good from you. His desire is to load you with His benefits – as we shall see later in this book.

From my personal study and experience in life and ministry, I have come to recognize and establish that, there are many different levels or dimensions of favour. In this chapter, I want us to take a good look at only three of them. It is my prayer that you will move from one level of favour unto another as you embark on an exciting journey of reading this chapter with me! The three levels of favour are as follows:

1. ELEMENTARY FAVOUR

THIS IS THE KIND OF FAVOUR THAT COMES ON ALL THOSE THAT LIVE RIGHTEOUSLY. I call this the elementary or general favour because it is available to, and granted to all righteous people. By righteous, I mean all who have a right standing with God. As long as you are born again and you have Christ living in you, this level and measure of favour is your portion to access and enjoy. It is your divine heritage. This dimension of favour grants the believer in Christ the opportunity and right to partake in the divine nature of God:

> *"Grace and peace be multiplied to you in the knowledge of God and of Jesus our Lord, as His divine power has given to us all things that pertain to life and godliness, through the knowledge of Him who called us by glory and virtue, by which have been given to us exceedingly great and precious promises, that through these **you may be***

partakers of the divine nature, *having escaped the corruption that is in the world through lust."*
(2 Peter 1: 2-4, NKJV)

Indeed, as a righteous person it is your right and privilege to possess, enjoy and walk in this favour each day of your life. If you are ignorant of this truth, you will live a favour-less life and go on struggling and going through so much stress in life. It is my prayer that every believer in Christ will catch this revelation and confess favour upon their lives each day as David did, when he declared in prayer:

"For surely, O Lord, you bless the righteous; you surround them with your favour as with a shield." (Psalm 5:12)

2. DISTINGUISHING FAVOUR

ONE DAY A GENTLEMAN CAME TO SEE ME AFTER A CHURCH SERVICE and told me he was going for an interview to secure his permanent stay in England. I laid my hands on him and declared that "may distinguishing favour follow you!" A very simple prayer! Now, some days later, I got a phone call and it was from him. He was so ecstatic with joy and he thanked me for the prayer I prayed over him before he went for the interview.

He explained that on the day of his interview, every one of the interviewees was refused their stay, except him. All glory be to God! This is what I call *distinguishing favour.*

This is the kind of favour that grants you notice among men and makes them single you out and do you good without knowing why they do so! Daniel walked in such kind of favour.

> *"For surely, O Lord, you bless the righteous; you surround them with your favour as with a shield."*
>
> **Psalm 5:12**

SHADRACH, MESHECH AND ABEDNEGO ALSO ENJOYED IT. Joseph enjoyed this special favour everywhere he worked. Even in prison, he was distinguished by favour and was made the captain over all his peers. Can you imagine a prisoner in chains, yet the one who gives instruction to all fellow prisoners! He was even a consultant to the prison officer in-charge and his fellows. David experienced this kind of favour even when he was a mere teenage shepherd.

GOD TOLD SAMUEL TO TELL JESSE: "We are not sitting down until he comes!" Can you imagine that! A mere shepherd boy who had been relegated to the background, yet when he came home, the prophet saluted him and bowed to him. Why? Because inside that smallish boy was Israel's best ever king! Inside that outwardly dirty boy was a great giant-slayer, Israel's greatest psalmist and warrior, and the only man in the Bible described by God as "the man after my own heart."

This is the kind of favour that comes on an individual and distinguishes him from others. An example of this is when several applications are sent to an office but only yours will be picked out. As you continue to read this book, may this kind of favour follow you wherever you go in Jesus' name! Amen.

> *"O Lord when you favoured me you made my mountain to stand firm or to stand out."*
> *(Psalm 30:7)*

3. HIGH FAVOUR

"WHEN THE ANGEL VISITED THE VIRGIN MARY HE SAID "Greetings, you who are highly favoured! The Lord is with you" (Luke 1:28). This is the kind of favour that comes upon a man and makes his success and achievements so great and unexplainable. For example, in Mary's case how could a woman conceive without having sexual intercourse with a man? This cannot be explained! That is why the Roman Catholics call it "Immaculate Conception." It was indeed a supernatural, perfect conception. It was the kind of conception that defied biological and genetical facts. She was still a pure virgin, yet by divine favour she found a growing baby in her womb!

Boakye, a young man without any academic qualification, was stranded on the streets of Ghana selling recharge cards. A man drove to him to ask for some assistance so Boakye willingly helped the man. After everything the man asked Boakye what he would want in return. Overwhelmed, Boakye just said "Anything." The man was touched by the kind gesture of Boakye and he enabled this uneducated guy secure an America visa to travel outside Ghana. As you read this book, this uneducated guy has become a successful businessman. He owns three companies and lives happily in America. This is what I call high favour. It can never be explained.

Have you received some huge gifts with no strings attached before? That is how 'high' favour operates; it causes actions to be taken without human logic protesting. How did you feel, knowing that you had the power and ability to be a blessing? Now, here is another angle: Have you ever done a favour for someone before, when after you did it you questioned the wisdom in what you just did? How do you think God feels when He shows you high favour in the form of His grace and goodness?

I want you to know that God does not always do things for you because you have done something for Him. So, anytime you receive a great blessing from God that you cannot explain, that is God's grace at work, and His grace is favour that we do not merit or earn. It is a free gift that overwhelms and humbles us – as the father of the Prodigal Son showed unto his son! When it comes to high favour, God does not expect you to do anything for Him or in return. Even your heartfelt gratitude is insufficient in

> *"Faith is a living, daring confidence in God's grace, so sure and certain that a man could stake his life on it a thousand times."*
>
> ~ MARTIN LUTHER

measure of the high favour from God. You cannot repay God even if you tried to, all your whole life on earth! That is why it is called 'high favour'.

YOU SEE, ONE DEFINITION OF 'GRACE' IS 'UNMERITED DIVINE ASSISTANCE.' This includes approval, favour, mercy, pardon and privilege. Grace is love exemplified. It was the divine impetus that compelled God the Father to send Jesus Christ onto the earth. He freely gave His Only Begotten Son because He wanted you. The Gospel (which means 'good news') is the blessing, the eternal promise of God's grace and favour.

GOD HAS GRANTED YOU A HIGHLY PRIVILEGED STATUS. You are His adopted child. He named you an Ambassador of His Kingdom. In addition, you have been granted Jesus' power of attorney to use His Name - the Name above all names. Jesus is King of kings and Lord of lords; and you are one of the kings and lords of which He is the Head. You are royalty! Kingship has power, right and status. You are 'seated in heavenly places' reigning with Christ Jesus. All the power of God is available to you through His Word, His grace and His favour.

CHAPTER 4

PEOPLE THAT ATTRACTED GOD'S FAVOUR IN THE BIBLE

"God favors men and women who delight in being made worthy of happiness before the happiness itself."

CRISS JAMI

Sometimes, the one favoured by God and man is shown kindness and treated with a generosity and goodwill far beyond what would normally be expected. This is generally the favour that we receive from the Lord. The more we please God, the more we will be favoured by Him. What we should understand therefore is that, the favour of God will often lead to the favour of men. Throughout the Bible there are some people that attracted God's favour and that favour connected them to great people who also favoured them. A few examples are mentioned below:

1. JOSEPH [GENESIS 39:21]

JOSEPH WAS FAVOURED BY GOD and God turned his captivity into coronation. It was favour that made him to be promoted from a prisoner to a Prime Minister, in the land he was supposed to be a slave and a prisoner! What a paradox! That is how God's favour makes way for favour before men to come your way, when you please God. May the same favour that followed Joseph be your portion now, in Jesus' name!

2. RUTH [BOOK OF RUTH]

RUTH WAS A FOREIGNER, but she had great favour before Boaz, a kinsman-redeemer from her late husband's family. God's favour orchestrated circumstances until ultimately, she got married to Boaz and became the mother of Jesse and the grandmother of David, who was in the bloodline of Jesus, our Saviour and Redeemer. It was favour that brought Ruth into the genealogy of Jesus Christ.

May this same favour follow you from today forward and connect you into your destiny and all people that God has destined to help you pursue and accomplish His purposes in your life. May you be so favoured that your legacy will be a lasting blessing to generations yet unborn, in Jesus' name!

3. ESTHER [ESTHER 2:17]

ESTHER FOUND FAVOUR WITH A FOREIGN KING and became the queen of the land. My advice goes to you, my dear single woman: are you ready and seeking for a man to marry you? What you need in order to get a good man is not necessarily the cosmetic make-up or the dresses you wear or the car you drive. Don't worry yourself spending so much money on styling your hair and putting on expensive clothing and perfume just to attract a man to you.

WHAT YOU NEED FOREMOST IS GOD'S FAVOUR! I am not saying that being fashionable and physically attractive is not good, but you do not put your trust in that. If you care to observe, more often than not, it is the most ordinary-looking women who tend to attract the best of men in the community or the church. The secret is favour and not fashion! So to you my dear lady reading this book, who is looking forward to marrying soon, may the same favour that came upon Esther follow you, as you pay the price of good preparation of the heart and character, in Jesus' Name!

4. JESUS CHRIST

THE FIRST MENTION OF FAVOUR IN THE NEW TESTAMENT IS LUKE 1:28-31. Here, Mary was approached by Angel Gabriel. His salutation heralded Mary's favoured status in the Throne Room. Notice in these verses that the word 'favour' is repeated twice. The word favour, from the Greek word *charis* (pronounced khar-ece), is a word revealing a two-fold process of the law of attraction. The first definition describes an attraction of God to you and the second describes the release of an influence through you that inclines other people to love you, trust you, like you and willing to assist you in your assignment in life.

For example, God was attracted to Mary because her heart's desire was toward Him. God was already seeking for a virgin whose heart was ready for Him to use as a vessel for His greatest act of love towards mankind. God found that heart in Mary and chose her above all the several thousands of damsels in Israel. That is what favour is: being singled out and to be preferred. It is God choosing you – who is least expecting - as His favourite among many who lobby for His attention.

DO YOU REMEMBER JOB'S CONFESSION that God gave him "life and favour"? Yes, surely you receive divine favour when you experience God's visitation. May this be your hour of visitation, my dear reader! I see God visiting you now and transforming you, changing your situation radically than you can ever imagine or expect! When God visits you, He leaves you radically different from how He met you. He did that to Jacob, when He wrestled with him as an Angel. By the time the strange encounter was over, the shameful name Jacob had been changed to Israel! In Mary's case, after the divine encounter, she was left pregnant of the Holy Child!

WHENEVER GOD VISITS YOU, HE IMPREGNATES YOU WITH A VISION; a daring dream, an assignment, and a mission. You may not understand it all at first, but once the favour of God comes, the assignment becomes more personal, passionate and compelling. When you spend prolonged time in God's awesome presence, you supernaturally conceive His dream and His desire. That is what favour means: conceiving God's goodness and goodwill to give birth later to a vision or a dream that brings glory to God as it delivers many from bondage and captivity.

GOD DOES NOT GRANT YOU FAVOUR FOR FAVOUR'S SAKE or for your personal gain. Anyone who receives God's favour receives also the favour before men in order to solve problems of humanity and God's people. When Hadassah was favoured, her name was changed to Queen Esther, and she was not made a Queen for nothing. God saw the ploy of Haman far ahead of time, and so planted Mordecai at the king's palace and through him, strategically positioned Esther as the Queen of Persia, and through her, God uprooted Haman and all his evil people and granted amnesty and redemption to His people, the Jews! May God favour you so you shall become His channel of redemption to those who need redemption!

GOD'S FAVOUR COMES IN DEGREES

THE MORE WE PLEASE GOD, THE MORE HE FAVOURS US. Therefore, just as we grow in the levels of anointing and different measures of grace, so do we grow and increase in favour. Dr. Luke revealed that about the Child Jesus: "And the Child grew and became strong in spirit, filled with wisdom; and the grace of God was upon Him...And Jesus increased in wisdom and stature, and in favour with God and men" (Luke 2:40, 52, NKJV). That means, from His childhood, the Lord increased in maturity in His spirit, soul and body. Apart from developing in all aspects of His life, the Lord Jesus increased in "favour with God and men."

You can also increase in the favour God has given you. As we shall read later, favour comes in different dimensions, degrees and levels. You can move from one dimension of favour unto the next higher level.

CHAPTER 5

FAVOUR, MERCY AND GRACE

"Grace is free sovereign favor to the ill-deserving."

- BENJAMIN B. WARFIELD

THERE IS A CLOSE ASSOCIATION BETWEEN THESE THREE: FAVOUR, GRACE AND MERCY. Grace gives you what you do not deserve but mercy stops what you deserve for wrong-doing from coming to you. Simply put, grace is God's unmerited favour. Grace is God doing good for us that we do not deserve. In the Bible, grace and mercy are like two heads of the same coin.

Mercy is God withholding judgment or evil that I deserve; grace is God giving me blessing or good that I do not deserve. Because of God's mercy, I do not receive the judgment of God against my sins; because of God's grace, I receive eternal life and a promise of heaven though I do not deserve them. Both mercy and grace come to me through the Lord Jesus Christ. Grace can also be defined as God's sufficiency or God's fullness in the life of the believer. God told Paul,

> *"My grace is sufficient for thee: for my strength is made perfect in weakness."*
> *(2 Corinthians 12:9)*

> *"The growth of grace is like the polishing of metals. There is first an opaque surface; by and by you see a spark darting out, then a strong light; till at length it sends back a perfect image of the sun that shines upon it."*
>
> **EDWARD PAYSON**
> **(1783-1827)**

That is, the grace of God in Paul enabled him and empowered him in his weakness. God's grace working in us supplies the sufficiency whereby we may abound to every good work. Indeed, grace indicates that our God is more than enough! By this I mean that God is enough for us, no matter what the situation we face. As long as God is by your side, His grace is sufficient to carry you through the flood, the fiery furnace, the 'valley of the shadow of death' and any form of adversity! Elaborating on this, Apostle Paul wrote:

> *"And God is able to make all grace abound toward you; that ye, always having all sufficiency in all things, may abound to every good work."*
> *(2 Corinthians 9:8)*

GRACE IS FIRST OF ALL NECESSARY FOR OUR SALVATION. Ephesians 2:8 states categorically: "For by grace are ye saved through faith; and that not of yourselves: it is the gift of God." One aspect of salvation is called justification. That is the act by which we are declared just or righteous before God on the basis of the payment Jesus Christ made for our sin with His shed blood. The Bible clearly teaches that we are justified by the grace of God

> *"...being justified freely by His grace through the redemption that is in Christ Jesus..." (Romans 3:24, NKJV)*

> *"...that having been justified by His grace we should become heirs according to the hope of eternal life." (Titus 3:7)*

Not only are we saved by the grace of God, we also serve the Lord and live the Christian life by the grace of God. The letters of Paul always speak of a blessing of grace for the believers, along with peace. For example, Romans 1:7 states categorically: "Grace to you and peace from God our Father, and the Lord Jesus Christ." Paul is speaking to believers who are already saved and on their way to heaven, but he also recognizes that they need grace for living the Christian life here on earth, as Paul testified,

> *"But by the grace of God I am what I am: and his grace which was bestowed upon me was not in vain; but I laboured more abundantly than*

they all: yet not I, but the grace of God which was with me."
(1 Corinthians 15:10)

It was God's grace that made Paul what he was. It was God's goodness working in Paul that made him the great servant of God that he was. So, obviously, we also need the grace of God. We need it first of all for salvation. Without the grace of God, we cannot have eternal life.

> *"For the grace of God that bringeth salvation hath appeared to all men."*
>
> *Titus 2:11*

However, we also need the grace of God for our daily walk with God. We are weak and prone to stray. Jesus told us that we can do nothing without Him (John 15:5). But God provides daily strength through His grace working in us. We should seek this grace for living from Him. Then, we should believe that He will provide what He has promised and walk with assurance that His grace is working in us.

DIFFERENCE BETWEEN GRACE AND MERCY

Grace and mercy are two of the most used words these days not only pertaining to the religious aspect. However, they are usually misunderstood as to how profound these two words are. Grace is often said to be a blessing that we do not necessarily deserve. In the scope of Christianity, this is defined as the love of God that has been bestowed to man, in spite of his own shortcomings and frailty to sin. It can also be described as the generosity that we get to receive albeit unexpectedly, maybe in part to asking a favour or just wishful thinking.

"Grace is given to heal the spiritually sick, not to decorate spiritual heroes."

MARTIN LUTHER KING, JR.

MERCY IS DEFINED AS compassion shown to someone who has done something wrong. It encompasses forgiveness in terms of someone doing an error and accepting the fault that was done either by oneself or by another person. It is an act in which one shows forbearance and kindness to someone. Mercy is giving out compassion to someone you have authority over.

"The law detects, grace alone conquers sin."

SAINT AUGUSTINE *OF HIPPO (354-430)*

GRACE IS UNMERITED FAVOUR, and it is purely done out of absolute love. These blessings come in ways that no amount of self sacrifice can make up to repay those gifts. Mercy, on the other hand, is considered as giving the provisions that someone deserves. It prevents one from receiving the expected negative effect of one's actions, even though one knows that one fully deserves it. Both are needed in terms of holistic existence and that they usually go together. These values are rooted in the long standing history of Christianity; these are also deeply rooted in the integral core of each person and are encouraged to be practised each day.

> *"For whoso findeth me findeth life, and shall, obtain favour of the Lord."*
>
> **Proverbs 8:35**

There was nothing whatsoever in the Lord Jesus to deserve such vile treatment from the hands of His enemies, nothing whatsoever that He had done warranting such awful enmity on their part. In like manner, there is nothing whatsoever in any sinner to call forth the favourable regard of a holy God, nothing done by him to win His love; instead, everything to the contrary. Grace, then, is gratis, a free gift.

The very expression "the grace of God" implies and denotes that the sinner's condition is desperate to the last degree and that God may justly leave him to perish; yea, it is a wonder of wonders that he is not already in hell. Grace is a divine provision for those who are so depraved they cannot change their own nature, so averse from God they will not turn to Him, so blind they can neither see their woe nor the remedy, so dead spiritually that God must bring them out of their graves on to resurrection ground if ever they are to walk in newness of life.

Grace is the sinner's last and only hope; if he is not saved by grace, he will never be saved at all. Grace levels all distinctions, and regards the most zealous religionist on the same plane as the most reckless, the chaste virgin as the foul prostitute. Therefore, God is perfectly free to save the chief sinners and bestow His mercy on the vilest of the vile.

According to A. W. Tozer (1897-1963),

> Grace is the good pleasure of God that inclines him to bestow benefits upon the undeserving. It is a self-existent principle inherent in the divine nature and appears to us as a self-caused propensity to pity the wretched, spare the guilty, welcome the outcast, and bring into favour those who were before under just disapprobation. Its use to us sinful men is to save us and make us sit together in heavenly places to demonstrate to the ages the exceeding riches of God's kindness to us in Christ Jesus.

FAVOUR IS ACTUALLY A PART OF GRACE

IN THE ENGLISH NEW TESTAMENT, the Word 'grace' and the word 'favour' are both translated from the same Greek word 'charis'. So **the grace of God is the favour of God** and **the favour of God is the grace of God**. It causes things to happen in our lives that need to happen through the channel of faith. His power is doing something for us that we can neither earn nor deserve. Think about that! **God wants to give you special privileges.** His favour will cause people to go out of their way to bless you without even knowing why they're doing it.

"Grace is available for each of us every day - our spiritual daily bread - but we've got to remember to ask for it with a grateful heart and not worry about whether there will be enough for tomorrow."

- SARAH BAN BREATHNACH

HOW DOES FAVOUR WORK? Favour makes things fall into the right place. Favour makes obstacles disappear! Yes, in the spiritual realm, they were already lined up with your name tagged on them. God caused those delays and detours just to prepare your character for the blessings that He was bringing your way. God knows that charisma must match character, and when your character is developed and conformed to Christ enough, the Father causes a divine accident: making you collide with His divine favour! Then it becomes as if, by accident, you just walked into those blessings!

"Favor is the special affection of God toward you that releases an influence on you, so that others are inclined to like you, or to cooperate with you."

- LANCE WALLNAU

God's **supernatural** favour flowing in your life is not based on your background, ethnicity, tribe, skin colour, creed, looks or personality. His favour is based on His Word and believing what it says about you. Favour can break through barriers set against you, and it is available to every believer.

GRACE IS NOT A LICENCE FOR SINNING

> *"Do you not know that all of us who have been baptized into Christ Jesus were baptized into his death? We were buried therefore with him by baptism into death, in order that, just as Christ was raised from the dead by the glory of the Father, we too might walk in newness of life. For if we have been united with him in a death like his, we shall certainly be united with him in a resurrection like his. We know that our old man was crucified with him in order that the body of sin might be brought to nothing, so that we would no longer be enslaved to sin. For one who has died has been set free from sin. Now if we have died with Christ, we believe that we will also live with him. We know that Christ, being raised from the dead, will never die again; death no longer has dominion over him. For the death he died he died to sin, once for all, but the life he lives he lives to God. So you also must consider yourselves dead to sin and alive to God in Christ Jesus."*
> *(Romans 6:3-11)*

What Paul was saying was that, it is not the intention of the Gospel to teach sin or to allow it; it teaches the very opposite: how we may escape from sin and from the awful wrath of God which it incurs. To do so, we need God's grace in order to overcome the power of sin. That is why Paul strongly commended the grace of Christ and its consolation (Romans 5:20), declaring that "where sin increased, grace abounded all the more," and that where there are many and great sins, there also reigns great, abundant and rich grace.

> *"As heat is opposed to cold, and light to darkness, so grace is opposed to sin."*
>
> **THOMAS BENTON BROOKS (1608-1680)**

ARE YOU DOWN IN SIN? Rise up, repent and run to the Lord for His grace and mercies. Tap into His love and hold onto the sceptre of favour He is pointing to you and be saved. Now that you are saved from the power of sin and fully pardoned, begin to walk in God's favour and turn your back to sin and unrighteousness. Choose to live for Christ, and He shall supply you more grace and favour to walk in His righteousness and goodwill!

CHAPTER 6

BENEFITS OF FAVOUR

"Thou shalt arise, and have mercy upon Zion: for the time to favour her, yea, the set time, is come!"

PSALM 102:13

BELOVED, WE ARE IN THE LAST DAYS, when the glory of the Lord shall cover all the earth! We His people are about to experience the greatest of revivals and God is saving the best for the last! We are favoured to be the ones to experience the favour of God in its fullness and in an unprecedented manner! So get ready and strategically position yourself, because there is going to be radical changes in your life and around your house! The set time to favour you has come!

> **"Thou shalt arise, and have mercy upon Zion: for the time to favour her, yea, the set time, is come!" (PSALM 102:13)**

> *"Remember me, O LORD, with the favour that thou bearest unto thy people: O visit me with thy salvation."*
>
> **PSALM 106:4**

I LOVE THE KEY PHRASE OF THE QUOTE ABOVE: A "SET TIME." That indicates that God has already set a programme in motion in the spiritual realms and when the time is due to implement it, no power, or authority or government can change it. It is a set time and already pre-programmed from heaven. Notice what this "set time" is for. Favour is to come upon Zion. Zion is always symbolic of the Church. In other words, there is a set time for favour to come upon the Church like it has never experienced before.

Remember we are reading the words of a prophet and so the words of the Psalm are prophetic. This time, David is not speaking as just a king or just a psalmist. He was seeing into the future. Verse 15 says, "So the heathen shall fear the name of the Lord and all the kings of the earth thy glory." The "age to come" that Paul spoke about in Ephesians 2:7 has come! Therefore, we should expect the favour of God on us like never before!

WE ARE ALSO IN THE SET TIME AND THAT IS WHAT WE MUST BE EXPECTING! Can you imagine how exciting this is going to be! God has saved the best for last! Now that we are at the set time, I want to share with you some major benefits of favour that I have located from God's Word, that He has preserved to all those who walk in His divine favour. These are benefits you can expect when the favour of God is on your life. Study each of these carefully and begin to confess them every day, in the morning, and when you are going to sleep at night. May God confirm His Word in your life as you boldly embrace it and declare it over your life. Let us examine the benefits of favour now.

1. WHEN GOD FAVOURS YOU, WEALTH BEGINS TO FLOW TO YOU

"Lift up thine eyes round about, and see: all they gather themselves together, they come to thee: thy sons shall come from far, and thy daughters shall be nursed at thy side." Then thou shall see, and flow together, and thine heart shall fear, and be enlarged; because the abundance of the sea shall be converted unto thee, the forces of the Gentiles shall come unto thee." (Isaiah 60:4-5)

In the Hebrew, the word "forces" is translated "wealth" and wealth is associated or connected to favour. When you study the Bible, you will see that many who walked in the favour of God experienced financial blessings as well. Favour produces wealth. God has prophesied that a financial abundance will take place in the earth before the appearing of the Lord Jesus, and that the wealth of the sinner has been laid up for the just. Therefore if this "set time" of favour has come, then the Church can expect greater wealth and finances!

This great harvest of wealth will be experienced by those who are faithful and living righteously for God. If you are one of those, then you are a candidate for greater financial favour than you have ever experienced before in your life! If you are a giver and a good tither, then get ready because God is about to pile wealth on those He can trust with money and great wealth! There is a pattern for this in II Chronicles 1:12, when Solomon was given the assignment to build the temple:

> *"Wisdom and knowledge is granted unto thee; and I will give thee riches, and wealth, and honour, (or favour) such as none of the kings have had that have been before thee, neither shall there any after thee have the like."*
> *(2 Chronicles 1:12)*

> *"And the king made silver and gold at Jerusalem as plenteous as stones..."*
> *(2 Chronicles 1:15)*

Can you imagine that! Having so much gold and silver that it is lining the street like gravel! The great sacrifices and prayer of Solomon overwhelmed God and God was so pleased with him that, later, in 2 Chronicles, He appeared in His glory:

> *"It came even to pass, as the trumpeters and singers were as one, to make one sound to be heard in praising and thanking the Lord: and when they lifted up their voice with the trumpets and cymbals and instruments of music and praised the Lord, saying, For he is good; for his mercy endureth for ever: that then the house was*

filled with a cloud, even the house of the Lord; So that the priests could not stand to minister by reason of the cloud for the glory of the Lord had filled the house of God." (2 Chronicles 5:13,14)

Indeed, the time to favour us has come and "When the Lord shall build up Zion, He shall appear in His glory" (Psalm 102:13, 16). Notice what precedes the appearing of the Lord: a "set time of favour." when Solomon built the temple, notice that, God granted him honour and favour, and with it came riches, wealth and honour. Not only that, but with it came the right people and all that he needed in abundance. God gave Solomon people of quality and of great expertise, talents, and anointing.

2. FAVOUR PRODUCES SUPERNATURAL INCREASE AND PROMOTION

"But the Lord was with Joseph, and shewed him mercy, and gave him favour in the sight of the keeper of the prison."
Genesis 39:21

3. FAVOUR PRODUCES RESTORATION OF EVERYTHING THAT THE ENEMY HAS STOLEN FROM YOU

"And I will give this people favour in the sight of the Egyptians: and it shall come to pass, that, when ye go, ye shall not go empty."
(Exodus 3:21)

4. FAVOUR PRODUCES HONOUR IN THE MIDST OF YOUR ADVERSARIES

"And the Lord gave the people favour in the sight of the Egyptians. Moreover the man Moses was very great in the land of Egypt, in the sight Pharaoh's servants, and in the sight of the people." (Exodus 11:3)

5. FAVOUR BRINGS DIVINE PROTECTION

The favour of God protected David.

"Surely, Lord, you bless the righteous; you surround them with your favour as with a shield. (Psalm 5:12)

6. FAVOUR FACILITATES ANSWERED PRAYERS

"Then Queen Esther answered, "If I have found favour with you, Your Majesty, and if it pleases you, grant me my life - this is my petition. And spare my people - this is my request." (Esther 7:3)

"Before they call I will answer; while they are still speaking I will hear." (Isaiah 65:24)

7. FAVOUR OPENS LOCKED DOORS

FAVOUR OPENS DOORS OF OPPORTUNITIES FOR YOU. It is the favour of God that has opened great doors for me in ministry and life. It is the favour of God that has opened doors for me to be able to advice people in high governmental positions. Every one of us needs favour to operate to our fullest potential. Favour is the attractive force that makes people like you or be eager to do business with you. God is the source of favour and when He favours a man, everything that is stale in life is transformed into a sweet-smelling aroma!

8. FAVOUR CAN BRING UNEXPECTED INCOME

The nation of Israel came out of bondage and received their back pay from working overtime for the Egyptians. The Hebrews didn't borrow anything. They took gold, silver, and jewels from the Egyptians. The scriptures reveal,

> *"The Lord gave the people favour in the sight of the Egyptians and they loaned the people such things as they required and the people spoiled the Egyptian." Exodus 12:36*

Later, in the wilderness, Moses received an offering for the building of the tabernacle. Much of the gold and precious metals used to build the house of God was given in an offering received by the man of God. The gold of the Egyptians became the wealth of the Hebrews and was used in the furniture of the tabernacle. This is a true example of the "wealth of the wicked being laid up for the just."

9. FAVOUR CAN BRING THE RIGHT COMPANION INTO YOUR LIFE

A great example of this is found in the story of Ruth. She had a lot working against her. She was a widow, a stranger in the land of Israel, and a Moabite. The Jews did not take kindly to the Moabites. In fact, a curse was placed upon them in Deuteronomy, up to the tenth generation. Yet, Ruth chose to make the break from her past, enter into a covenant with the Hebrew God, and allow God to direct her path.

When she met Boaz, she saw the man of her dreams. Ruth said to Boaz, *"Let me find favour in thy sight..."* (Ruth 2:13). Boaz allowed Ruth to glean in his barley field to help supply her and Naomi's needs. She obtained favour, and he gave her handfuls of grain on purpose (Ruth 2:6). Afterwards, he gave her six measures of grain (Ruth 3:15). Finally she had his attention, and Boaz married her! From their marriage came Obed, the father of Jesse, who was the father of King David (Ruth 4:18-22).

When you have prayed for favour and direction, you need not chase some man or woman around trying to get their attention. The favour of God can act like a magnet and attract the right person into your life.

10. FAVOUR CAN STOP A NATIONAL DISASTER

When the Jews were in Persia, a wicked man named Haman set out to destroy the entire nation. Haman was an Aggagite, meaning he was a descendant of King Agag. This Canaanite king was ruling in the time of Saul and was the king of the Amalekites. In Saul's time, Agag was slain by the prophet Samuel. Therefore, Haman was full of revenge and chose to destroy the Jews in Persia as retaliation against them for the death of his ancestors.

The plot would have succeeded, had not Queen Esther made a decision to appear before the king. This sounds simple. The queen always had access to the king; but not in Persia. The king had gotten rid of his previous wife because she showed him disrespect, and a law had been passed concerning the wives in the kingdom. Esther could have been killed for coming into the king's chamber without permission. Esther 2:17 reads,

> *"When the King saw Esther standing in the court she obtained favour in his sight."*

Five times the Bible mentions how Esther received favour in the sight of the king. Esther had good looks going for her, and the Lord used this to get the king's attention and his favour.

11. FAVOUR CAN BRING THE MIRACLE BIRTH OF A CHILD

Many barren women in the Bible conceived after a visitation from God. Yet, one received a child and certainly wasn't expecting or asking for it. Mary was engaged to Joseph and was a pure virgin. When Gabriel appeared to her, the angel announced,

> *"Fear not Mary...you have found favour with God..." (Luke 1:30)*

Under the Old Covenant, barrenness was considered a sign of the disfavour of God. This is why Hannah became bitter in her spirit and began travailing before God for a son (1 Samuel 1). Hannah's prayers were so intense; they moved the heart of God toward her. Instead of one son, she bore seven children (1 Samuel 2:5). Any barren woman reading this now, may the Lord favour you with twins, in the name of Jesus. Amen.

12. FAVOUR PRODUCES SUPERNATURAL INCREASE AND PROMOTION

One day a man walked to me after an anointing service and told me he had been jobless for over five years and that he was due for an interview in a company the following day. I joined him in prayer and I declared that may the anointing he had received that evening bring favour to him. God being so good, this man who had been jobless, after the interview received news that he had been offered the position as general manager of the company. The truth is that he went for the interview seeking the position of an assistant Human Resource manager. This is what favour can do. May you receive supernatural promotion right now in Jesus' name.

> *"But the Lord was with Joseph, and showed him mercy, and gave him favour in the sight of the keeper of the prison."*
> *(Genesis 39:21)*

13. FAVOUR PRODUCES RESTORATION OF EVERYTHING THAT THE ENEMY HAS STOLEN FROM YOU

> *"And I will give this people favour in the sight of the Egyptians: and it shall come to pass, that, when ye go, ye shall not go empty."*
> *(Exodus 3:21)*

14. FAVOUR PRODUCES HONOUR IN THE MIDST OF YOUR ADVERSARIES

> *"And the Lord gave the people favour in the sight of the Egyptians. Moreover the man Moses was very great in the land of Egypt, in the sight of Pharaoh's servants, and in the sight of the people." (Exodus 11:3)*

15. FAVOUR PRODUCES GREAT VICTORIES IN THE MIDST OF GREAT IMPOSSIBILITIES

"For it was of the Lord to harden their hearts, that they should come against Israel in battle, that he might destroy them utterly, and that they might have no favour, but that he might destroy them, as the Lord commanded Moses."
(Joshua 11:20)

16. FAVOUR PRODUCES RECOGNITION, EVEN WHEN YOU SEEM THE LEAST LIKELY TO RECEIVE IT

"And Saul sent to Jesse, saying, Let David, I pray thee, stand before me; for he hath found favour in my sight." (1 Samuel 16:22)

17. FAVOUR PRODUCES PROMINENCE AND PREFERENTIAL TREATMENT

"And the king loved Esther above all the women, and she obtained grace and favour in his sight more than all the virgins; so that he set the royal crown upon her head, and made her queen instead of Vashti."
(Esther 2:17)

18. FAVOUR CAUSES RULES AND LAWS TO BE CHANGED AND REVERSED TO YOUR ADVANTAGE

"And said, If it please the king, and if I have found favour in his sight, and the thing seem right before the king, and I be pleasing in his eyes, let it be written to reverse the letters devised by Haman the son of Hammedatha the Agagite, which he wrote to destroy the Jews which are in all the king's provinces."
(Esther 8:5)

19. FAVOUR MAKES GOD FIGHT OUR BATTLES FOR US

"For they got not the land in possession by their own sword, neither did their own arm save them: but thy right hand, and thine arm, and the light of thy countenance, because thou hadst a favour unto them."
(Psalm 44:3)

THESE ARE SOME MAJOR BENEFITS FOR YOUR PERUSAL. The Psalmist declared that we are compassed about by the favour of God. One translation says, "It surrounds us." Henceforth, when you get up every morning, anticipate the favour of God going before you. Anticipate the favour of God surrounding you. Expect favour to open doors for you, wherever you go. Expect these benefits of favour to manifest in your life.

REMEMBER YOU WILL GET EXACTLY WHAT YOU EXPECT. If you expect God's favour to surround you, then you will see it. If you don't, then it won't. Your expectations are more powerful than any negative thing that Satan can put before you. They will override the negative no matter how often they may manifest in your life. Expect God's favour in your life and the radical transformation your life will go through! Watch what favour will do in your life. The set time has come, so tap into it!

CHAPTER 7

REMAINING IN THE FAVOUR OF GOD

"Now plead with God to be gracious to us. With such offerings from your hands, will he accept you?" says the LORD Almighty."

MALACHI 1:19, NIV

THE TRUTH ABOUT FAVOUR IS THAT, there is nothing to be done to obtain it. This is because it comes freely from God. He is the Father in heaven and all good and perfect gifts come from Him. Nonetheless, there are certain things to do to remain in favour. What I mean is, you can lose favour with God. Yes, there are things that when you do, you position yourself outside the will of God and His favour zone.

A classic Old Testament example was King Saul. He found great favour with God and God located him and placed him on the throne as Israel's first king, when he least expected it. Yet later on, he became familiar with God and took His favour upon him for granted. He was not able to maintain the favour God granted him because of his disobedience. He chose to offer sacrifices, when God wanted his complete obedience. Because of this, God took His eyes from Saul and found a humble young man called David, whom He addressed as "a man after My own heart." This should serve as a caution to you and me today. May we never take God's abundant grace, goodness and favour for granted!

GOD BLESSES ALL WHO WALK IN FAITHFULNESS

GOD BLESSES THOSE WHO WALK IN FAITHFULNESS and He shows favour to those who favour Him! How do nations, communities, families and individuals lose the blessing and favour of God? There are many ways. I cite the example of prophet Haggai here. God inspired him to speak to Israel's backsliding status, and the first reason he listed was that of self-interests, which replace God's interests, when God's people choose to take His blessings and favour for granted. This was what he wrote about the ungrateful attitude of Israel:

> *"The time has not come, the time that the Lord's house should be built." (Haggai 1:2)*

The Israelites had given up the building of the Lord's house and instead chose to build their own houses. This scene took place sixty-eight years after King Solomon's temple was destroyed. A remnant had returned to Jerusalem out of Babylonian captivity specifically to rebuild God's house. And, indeed, they laid the foundation of the temple with passion and excitement!

But soon, they were met with difficulties and discouragement. Slowly, they lost interest in building God's house, and began to give excuses, saying, "This just isn't the time to build God's house. We are having too many problems, and besides, we are spending so much time here on God's work that we are neglecting our families and businesses!"

One by one, they all walked away to look after their own interests. The Lord's interests that had everything to do with their own well-being and continual receiving of favour became secondary on their agenda. They began building their own houses and they used the lumber that had been stored up for building the temple. How do believers today lose the blessing and favour of God? By stopping work on His temple!

THIS IS STILL HAPPENING TODAY!

IT HAPPENS WHEN WE STOP PRAYING and seeking God - when we stop building up His spiritual body! Haggai points out this problem: When the people put God's interests first, He provided their food and shelter. Indeed, they were cared for by Him in every way. Their vineyards grew, their grapes were heavy; they slept peacefully at night and their children danced in the streets. None of their enemies prevailed against them. It was a marvellous time of God's blessing but then the people became absorbed with their own self-interests!

> *"We urge you not to receive God's grace in vain. For he says, "In the time of my favour I heard you, and in the day of salvation I helped you." I tell you, now is the time of God's favour, now is the day of salvation."*
>
> 2 Corinthians 6:1,2

Our world is consumed with selfishness of all kinds, including self-pride, self-ambition, and self-will. Everyone seeks his own interests. Unfortunately, many Christians are also caught up in these temptations of being ungrateful to the God who had favoured us greatly with His grace and mercies. God, the loving Father, is saying, "I called for a drought on the land...and on all the labour of your hands." (Haggai 1:11). He is saying, "I want you to put My interests first, so I can again bless you and favour you!"

May we repent and turn back to God and receive His favour again and walk in His double favour! How can we turn back from our carnal and wicked ways? How can we return to God's love, which is our first love? How can we go back and walk in the arena of God's favour? Below are some few actions I suggest we can take to obey God in order to return to His love and to remain in His favour, all the rest of the days of our lives. Let us examine them now.

1. READ THE BIBLE, KEEP GOD'S COMMANDMENTS AND WALK IN OBEDIENCE.

"My son, do not forget my law, But let your heart keep my commands; for length of days and long life and peace they will add to you. Let not mercy and truth forsake you; Bind them around your neck, Write them on the tablet of your heart, and so find favour and high esteem in the sight of God and man. Trust in the Lord with all your heart, and lean not on your own understanding; in all your ways acknowledge Him, And He shall direct your paths." (Proverbs 3:1-6)

2. ENGAGE IN PROACTIVE CONFESSIONS OF GOD'S FAVOUR.

When you wake up every day, make positive confessions of God's favour upon your life and upon your family. Declare what you desire to see as you move out into the world of business, work or ministry.

3. EXERCISE MERCY ON OTHERS.

"Good understanding gains favour, but the way of the unfaithful is hard."
(Proverbs 13:15)

4. WALK IN HOLINESS AND RIGHTEOUSNESS.

The purpose of God's favour is to reconcile Man to Himself. God's reason for sending His Son Jesus Christ to the earth is to bring the fallen man back to Him and to the Eden life that Adam used to enjoy; a life full of peace and favour of God. God, therefore, seeks to help Man return to Him and to walk in His righteousness and holiness. So as you choose to please God by giving your life wholly to Him, I see God release His favour all over you!

> *"For You, O LORD, will bless the righteous; with favour You will surround him as with a shield." (Psalm 5:12)*

> *"Fools mock at sin, but among the upright there is favour." (Proverbs 14:9)*

5. CONTINUE TO ACKNOWLEDGE THE TOTAL DEPENDENCE ON GOD FOR HIS FAVOUR.

MY DEAR FRIEND, NEVER RELY ON YOUR HUMAN QUALIFICATIONS or attributes. Put your trust in God only and lean not on your own understanding. Proverbs 3:5 tells us: "Trust in the Lord with all your heart and lean not to your own understanding." This is probably one of the most difficult instructions to follow as humans. We always try to handle things on our own and leave God totally out of the mix. But if we would just trust in the God who made us, who loves us and has our absolute best interest at heart, we would be so much better off.

As humans, we are often depending on our limited knowledge. But the Bible tells us clearly not to depend or lean on that limited understanding. We need to trust in God's infinite knowledge and understanding. Never try to figure things out and go your own way. Instead, put your trust in the One who knows best. God will never leave you nor forsake you. He loves you unconditionally. He is always on time and all the time, He cares about everything you do and everything you are going through.

AS HUMANS, SOMETIMES IT IS SO HARD TO TRUST GOD. That is because we limit Him to the way we think. But Isaiah 55:8-9 tells us that God's thoughts are not our thoughts nor are His ways our ways. God does not operate or think with limitations. Things may seem impossible for us, but there is nothing that God cannot do! That is why King Solomon with all of his wisdom, told us to "Trust in the Lord with all of our heart." He knew that we would not be able to see our way through difficulties, problems, troubles and trials without the direction of our heavenly Father.

After Solomon told us to trust the Lord and not lean on what we know, he then told us to acknowledge God. He wrote in Proverbs 3:6, **"In all your ways acknowledge Him and He will direct your paths."** We need to make a conscious effort to tell God that we need Him. Acknowledge that He is the One who can make things right. Then the Bible says that He will direct our paths. If we will trust God, and not ourselves, and acknowledge Him, He will give us the guidance we need to succeed in life. He will help us and favour us beyond our wildest imagination. So my dear friend, keep on trusting God and most assuredly, He will never let you down!

Conclusion

MAY THE LORD GRANT YOU FAVOUR!

"Let not mercy and truth forsake thee: bind them about thy neck; write them upon the table of thine heart: So shalt thou find favour and good understanding in the sight of God and man."

Proverbs 3:3-4

GOD BLESS YOU FOR COMING THIS FAR WITH ME IN THIS BOOK! How do you feel now? I am sure you are feeling the wind of favour blowing all over you now, I do! Now that you have received favour, you have supernatural advantage for a successful life today than ever before! I assure you that, God wants you to succeed in every area of your life and with His presence in your life, you can. Yes, you can!

God's grace or unmerited favour can swing open doors of opportunities and locate you at the right places at the right time for His blessings. Even if you lack the necessary qualifications, looks and advantage, God's unmerited favour can propel you forward to higher grounds of promotion and great success!

As you have read this book, I know you have discovered the unmerited favour that only God gives to His beloved (and you are one) and how everything that you touch can be blessed and how you can enjoy good success. I am sure you have learnt about what Jesus has accomplished on the cross for you, and how, through His perfect sacrifice, you can lead an overcoming life as God's beloved.

> *"Let us therefore come boldly to the throne of grace, that we may obtain mercy and find grace to help in time of need."*
>
> **Hebrews 4:16**

Packed with new covenant truths on the unmerited favour of God and how you already have access to it through Jesus' finished work, this book has offered you the basis to trust in God and seek His face for His kind of favour to live the good life, God's way. It is time for you to stop depending on your own efforts to succeed and to start depending on Jesus and Jesus alone for every success. Start living out the dreams that God has birthed in your heart today!

NOW DECLARE GOD'S PROMISES OF FAVOUR OVER YOU!

BELOVED, THERE IS SO MUCH POWER IN THE WORDS WE SPEAK. What we say today creates the tomorrow we desire! If we want a healthy and prosperous future, then we need to use wisdom and speak words that bring positive results. Our future depends on it. To declare means: "to make known formally or officially." It means "to state emphatically or authoritatively or affirm". It also means "to reveal or make manifest; show." God spoke or declared all things into existence. Since we are created in His image He has given us the authority and the power to declare over our own lives, His promises and what we desire, based on His Word.

YOU MIGHT BE DECLARING OVER YOUR LIFE WITHOUT EVEN KNOWING IT. Have you ever said, "I hate my life", or "I'm so fat and ugly"? These are negative declarations that will bring negative results into your life. Change your words and begin to declare only positive words over your life. Begin to declare words that attract favour from God and from men that God causes to favour you and you will see the changes! The Bible tells us,

> *"So then faith comes by hearing, and hearing by the word of God." (Romans 10:17, NKJV)*

THE BIBLE IS A VERY POWERFUL TOOL we should use to declare God's Word over our lives. For example, I love to pray Psalm 91 over me time after time. You can do same.

Substitute "you" or "your" with "I, me, and my", as follows:

> *"Those who live in the shelter of the Most High will find rest in the shadow of the Almighty. This I declare about the LORD: He alone is my refuge, my place of safety; He is my God, and I trust him. For he will rescue me from every trap and protect me from deadly disease. He will cover me with his feathers. He will shelter me with his wings. His faithful promises are my armor and protection. I will not be afraid of the terrors of the night, nor the arrow that flies in the day. I will not dread the disease that stalks in darkness, nor the disaster that strikes at midday. Though a thousand fall at my side, though ten thousand are dying around me, these evils will not touch me. Just open my eyes, and I will see how the wicked are punished. If I make the LORD my refuge, if I make the Most High my shelter, no evil will conquer me; no plague will come near my home. For he will order his angels to protect me wherever I go. They will hold me up with their hands so I won't even hurt my foot on a stone. I will trample upon lions and cobras; I will crush fierce lions and serpents under my feet! The LORD says, "I will rescue those who love me. I will protect those who trust in my name. When they call on me, I will answer; I will be with them in trouble. I will rescue and honor*

> *them. I will reward them with a long life and give them my salvation."*
> *(Psalm 91, NLT)*

I also do the same for Ephesians 1:17-23 and Ephesians 3:14-21. Try that also and see:

> *"...asking God, the glorious Father of our Lord Jesus Christ, to give me spiritual wisdom and insight so that I might grow in my knowledge of God. I pray that my heart will be flooded with light so that I can understand the confident hope he has given to those he called—his holy people who are his rich and glorious inheritance."*
>
> *I also pray that I will understand the incredible greatness of God's power for us who believe him. This is the same mighty power that raised Christ from the dead and seated him in the place of honour at God's right hand in the heavenly realms. Now he is far above any ruler or authority or power or leader or anything else—not only in this world but also in the world to come. God has put all things under the authority of Christ and has made him head over all things for the benefit of the church. And the church is his body; it is made full and complete by Christ, who fills all things everywhere with himself." (Ephesians 1:17-23)*

"I pray that from his glorious, unlimited resources he will empower me with inner strength through his Spirit. Then Christ will make his home in my heart as I trust in him. My roots will grow down into God's love and keep me strong. And may I have the power to understand, as all God's people should, how wide, how long, how high, and how deep his love is. May I experience the love of Christ, though it is too great to understand fully. Then I will be made complete with all the fullness of life and power that comes from God. Now all glory to God, who is able, through his mighty power at work within me, to accomplish infinitely more than I might ask or think. Glory to him in the church and in Christ Jesus through all generations forever and ever! Amen."
(Ephesians 3:14-21)

> *"Nothing splendid has ever been achieved except by those who dared believe that something inside of them was superior to circumstance."*
>
> **Bruce Barton**

HOW DO YOU FEEL AFTER MAKING SUCH POWERFUL DECLARATIONS of God's blessings and favour upon your life? I know you feel so good! Surely, these awesome Bible verses shall begin to work in you and over your life now! Keep making more of such declarations with other promises of God from His Word and His favour shall continue to flow into your life. May

The Lord cause His face to shine upon you and make your way prosperous and make good success be your portion in all you do for His glory!

Pray This Prayer With Me Now:

For surely, O Lord, you bless the righteous. I, therefore, declare that I am blessed through Jesus Christ. Thank You for surrounding me with Your favour as with a shield. I thank You, Lord, that I can abound in your favour and blessing today. I, therefore, expect Your favour to go before me today. I anticipate the favour of God surrounding me and I expect my Heavenly Father to give me favour with men, even with the ungodly.

I thank You Heavenly Father for opening doors for me that neither man nor the devil can shut. Thank You for blessing the works of my hands as I walk under an open heaven. May I experience your supernatural increase and provision in every area of my life this day. I choose to walk in faith and in victory!

IN JESUS' NAME I PRAY! AMEN!

STEPS TO SALVATION

Maybe as you read this book, you may have lost your spiritual and Christian life or perhaps you have not accepted Jesus as your lord and personal savior. I have good news for you; no matter the sin you have committed, the blood of Jesus can wash you now and make you white as snow, only if you will believe.

If you would like to accept Jesus Christ as your lord and personal savior, It is very simple, say the prayer below and believe in your heart.

Lord Jesus, I thank you for my life, I thank you that you came to die just for me. I acknowledge that I am a sinner. Please, lord, forgive me and write my name in the book of life. I accept you into my heart right now, in Jesus name, AMEN.

If you prayed this prayer from your heart, you are now a born again Christian. Please find a Bible-believing church in your area and be part of the family of God.

BECOME A COVENANT PARTNER WITH BRIAN JONES OUTREACH MINISTRY

I invite you to become a partner in fulfilling the vision God has given us to reach the world with the gospel and also help the needy in cash and in kind in order to accomplish the great commission.

To become a covenant partner, simply simply contact us.

Our contact details
UK: (+44)75 560 60 924
Ghana: (+233) 24 114 795 3
Email: brianjonesoutreachministries@yahoo.co.uk

www.ingramcontent.com/pod-product-compliance
Lightning Source LLC
Chambersburg PA
CBHW071409040426
42444CB00009B/2170